Peru's Mountains

USING EARTH'S RESOURCES

Moana Ashley

PICTURE CREDITS
Cover: Huscaran Volcano and Rio Santa Valley © Charles & Josette Lenars/Corbis/Tranz; copper mine © Carl & Ann Purcell/ Corbis/Tranz.

page 1 © Kevin Schafer/Image Bank/Getty Images; page 4 (bottom left) © Wayne Lawler; Ecoscene/Corbis/Tranz; page 4 (bottom right) © Wolfgang Kaehler/Corbis/Tranz; page 5 (top) © Hubert Stadler/Corbis/Tranz; page 5 (bottom left), Photodisc; page 5 (bottom right) © Jim Zuckerman/Corbis/Tranz; page 6 © Galen Rowell/Corbis/Tranz; page 8 © Brian A. Vikander/ Corbis/Tranz; page 11 © Galen Rowell/Corbis/Tranz; page 12 © Peter Harholdt/Corbis/Tranz; page 13 © Champion Photography Ltd./Stock Image Group; page 15 © Michael & Patricia Fogden/ Corbis/Tranz; page 16, Digital Vision; page 21 © Jack Fields/ Corbis/Tranz; page 22 © Tim Scoones and Oxford Scientific Films/Hedgehog House; page 23 © AP/Fotopress; page 24 © Ric Ergenbright/Corbis/Tranz; page 25 © Peter Guttman/Corbis/Tranz; page 26 © courtesy of J. M. Micaud/14383/FAP; page 29, Brand X Pictures.

Produced through the worldwide resources of the National Geographic Society, John M. Fahey, Jr., President and Chief Executive Officer; Gilbert M. Grosvenor, Chairman of the Board; Nina D. Hoffman, Executive Vice President and President, Books and Education Publishing Group.

PREPARED BY NATIONAL GEOGRAPHIC SCHOOL PUBLISHING
Ericka Markman, Senior Vice President and President, Children's Books and Education Publishing Group; Steve Mico, Vice President and Editorial Director; Marianne Hiland, Executive Editor; Richard Easby, Editorial Manager; Jim Hiscott, Design Manager; Kristin Hanneman, Illustrations Manager; Matt Wascavage, Manager of Publishing Services; Sean Philpotts, Production Manager.

EDITORIAL MANAGEMENT
Morrison BookWorks, LLC

PROGRAM CONSULTANTS
Dr. Shirley V. Dickson, Program Director, Literacy, Education Commission of the States; James A. Shymansky, E. Desmond Lee Professor of Science Education, University of Missouri-St. Louis.

National Geographic Theme Sets program developed by Macmillan Education Australia, Pty Limited.

Published by the National Geographic Society
1145 17th Street, N.W.
Washington, D.C. 20036-4688

ISBN: 978-0-7922-4765-4
ISBN: 0-7922-4765-5

Printed in China

12 13 14 15 16 17 18 19 20 21
10 9 8 7 6 5

Contents

Using Earth's Resources

Nature provides people with many useful things. Air, water, plants, animals, minerals, and fuels all come from nature. Things that come from nature are called natural resources. Natural resources are found everywhere on Earth. They are found in the rain forests of Indonesia, the ocean region of Greenland, the deserts of Australia, and the mountains of Peru.

 ## Key Concepts ....

1. Earth provides many natural resources that people can use.
2. Different resources are useful to people in different ways.
3. Conservation and recycling can help save resources.

Four Resource-Rich Regions

Tropical Rain Forests

The trees in Indonesia's rain forests have many important uses.

Oceans

The oceans around Greenland teem with marine animals.

In this book you will learn about the resources found in Peru's mountains.

Deserts

The deserts of Australia provide people with fuels and minerals.

Mountains

The mountains of Peru offer a wealth of useful trees and minerals.

Mountain Resources

Imagine standing on a mountain slope surrounded by cool, moist forest. Around you, misty clouds sit low among the trees. Water drips from trees and other plants and joins the streams and rivers flowing downhill. As you make your way to the foothills of the mountain, you step into warm tropical rain forest. The temperature rises and the humidity builds. However, cross to the other side of the mountain range and you will find yourself in dry, rugged desert with little plant life. These are the Andes Mountains of Peru, one of the richest and most diverse regions on Earth.

Earth's Mountains

Mountains are landforms that stand higher than the areas around them. There are mountains on every one of Earth's continents. The climate in the higher regions of mountains is usually cold. Many mountains provide people with useful materials. They also affect Earth's climate and rainfall.

The Peruvian Andes

Peru and the Andes Mountains

Peru is a country along the Pacific coast in western South America. The entire country is located in the **tropics**, the region that lies between the Tropic of Cancer and the Tropic of Capricorn. The high ranges of the Andes Mountains run close to the western coast of the country.

High on the mountains, above 1,980 meters (6,500 feet), are grassy plateaus and snow-capped peaks. A little lower down on the eastern slopes are moist cloud forests. These forests are covered with clouds formed by the cooler temperatures in the high **altitudes**. At the foothills of the eastern slopes are tropical rain forests. In contrast, the western slopes of Peru's Andes are dry and rugged. They descend into a desert along the coast.

Look at the map. It shows where Peru's Andes Mountains are located.

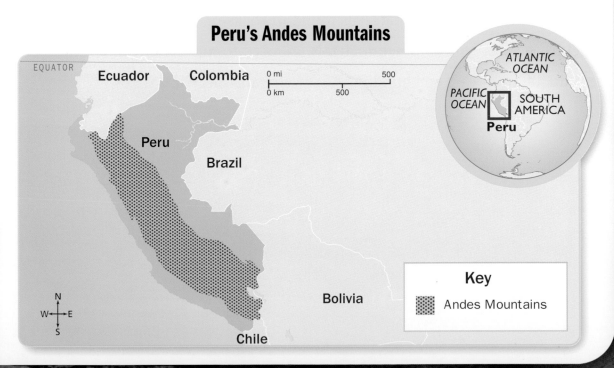

Peru's Andes Mountains

EQUATOR

Ecuador Colombia

0 mi   500
0 km   500

Peru

Brazil

ATLANTIC OCEAN

PACIFIC OCEAN   SOUTH AMERICA

Peru

Bolivia

N W E S

Chile

Key
Andes Mountains

Natural Resources

Mountains can provide people with important **natural resources**. Natural resources are materials found in nature that are useful to people. Everything that people use is either a natural resource in its raw form or produced from natural resources.

> natural resources
> materials that are found in nature and are useful to people

There are several different kinds of natural resources. Trees are one example of a useful natural resource found on many mountains. Trees are used to build houses and furniture and to make paper. Trees also provide people with other useful products, such as medicines and foods.

Minerals are also important natural resources often found in mountain areas. Minerals are solid materials found in rocks or beneath the ground. Metals are one type of mineral. Metals are used to make many different products, from cars and buildings to jewelry and electrical wires.

Trees are a natural resource found in Peru's mountains.

Resources from the Mountains

Peru's mountains provide people with many important natural resources. The main resources are trees and minerals. People use trees from both the cloud forests and the rain forests to make many different products. Mahogany, oak, and cedar trees from the cloud forests are logged, or cut down, and used for their timber. The bark of cinchona, quisuar, and quenual trees from the rain forests are used to make medicines. The trees from the rain forest also are sources of food such as bananas and pineapples.

The highlands of the mountains are rich in mineral **deposits**. Metals such as gold, copper, silver, lead, and zinc are found there. Like most other minerals, these metals are extracted from the ground by mining, or digging into the earth with special equipment. Peru has a huge mining industry that mines and exports large quantities of these metals.

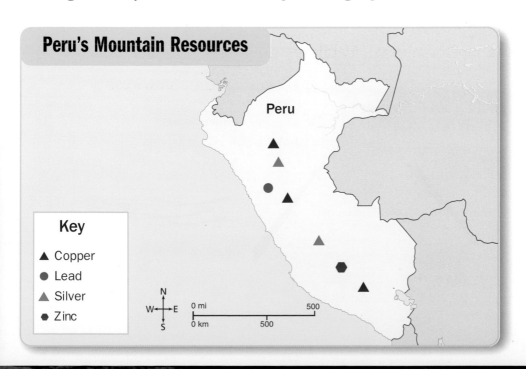

Peru's Mountain Resources

Peru

Key

▲ Copper
● Lead
▲ Silver
● Zinc

N
W—E
S

0 mi   500
0 km   500

Mountains and Rainfall

Mountains such as the Andes affect the climate of the region around them. This is because mountains act as barriers to the flow of air across Earth's surface.

When moving air, or wind, reaches the side of a mountain, it rises to move over the mountain. The air becomes cooler as the altitude increases. Water vapor in the air forms clouds. Rain falls on the side of the mountain where the air is rising, called the windward side. When the air passes over the top and reaches the other side of the mountain, or the leeward side, it descends. The leeward side remains dry because all the moisture has fallen as rain on the windward side.

In Peru, air generally moves from east to west. So the east side of the Andes, the windward side, has high rainfall. The west side, or leeward side, has very little rain. Most of the forests grow on the wet east side of the mountain.

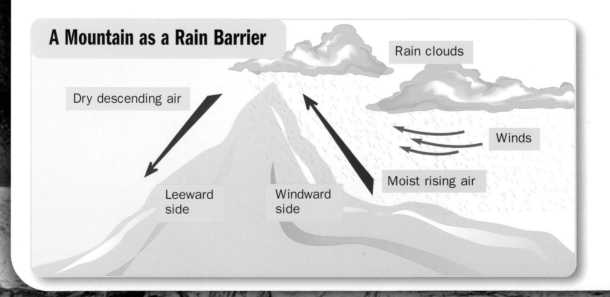

A Mountain as a Rain Barrier

Rain clouds

Dry descending air

Winds

Moist rising air

Leeward side

Windward side

How Mountain Resources Are Used

There are many different natural resources in the mountains of Peru. People use these natural resources in different ways. Most resources have their own unique **properties**, or qualities that make them different from other resources. The two most important resources in the mountains of Peru are trees and minerals.

The trees and minerals in Peru's mountains all have different properties and uses. For example, some trees may have hard wood while others may have soft wood. Some may have medicinal uses while others do not. Some metals may absorb a great amount of heat while others may absorb less. The special properties of a natural resource determine how the resource is used.

Salt is a mineral mined in the Peruvian Andes.

Timber   Several kinds of trees found on the forested slopes of the Peruvian Andes are used for their timber. These include mahogany, oak, and cedar. Wood from mahogany trees is attractive, strong, and hard, making it excellent for furniture. Oak wood is heavy and strong, and is used to make furniture and railroad ties. Peruvian cedar wood is very resistant to rot. This makes it good for building outdoor decks, boats, and furniture.

Furniture made from mahogany is strong and heavy.

Medicines   Other trees found in the forests of the Andes are used to make medicines. People use the bark of the cinchona tree to prepare **quinine**, a medicine used to treat the disease malaria.

The quisuar tree also provides a useful remedy. Local people use water boiled with parts of the tree to clean blisters.

The quenual tree grows at higher altitudes than any other tree in the world. It is found as high as 3,800 meters (12,500 feet) on the Andes. Local people chew the bark of this tree to prevent tooth decay. They also use the bark to dye cloth.

Metals The main metals obtained from the Peruvian Andes are copper and gold. Peru is one of the world's leading producers of copper, a pink-brown metal that is an excellent **conductor** of electricity. Because of this property, copper is used to make electrical wires and other electrical parts, such as television and computer parts. Copper also does not rust easily, so many objects that get wet, such as plumbing parts, are made from copper.

Copper is used to make electrical wires.

Copper can also be mixed with other metals to form an **alloy**. For example, copper is mixed with tin to form a strong alloy called bronze. Bronze is used to make parts for cars and heavy machines.

Gold is a **malleable**, or soft, yellow metal that never rusts or stains. Gold is rare, which makes it special and expensive. Because it is malleable, gold is often mixed with other metals such as silver or copper to make it harder. It is then made into jewelry. Gold can also be pressed into a thin sheet called "gold leaf" and used to line book edges and picture frames.

Peru ranks seventh among the world's gold-producing countries. Gold accounts for nearly 40 percent of Peru's mining exports. Many gold mines are located along the slopes of the Peruvian Andes.

Key Concept 3 Conservation and recycling can help save resources.

Using Earth's Resources Wisely

The mountains provide people with many useful natural resources. However, this supply of natural resources is not endless, and some resources have been **depleted**. People need to use natural resources wisely to ensure they do not run out.

There are two kinds of resources on Earth – **renewable** resources and **nonrenewable** resources. Renewable resources are resources that are **replenished** soon after they have been used, such as water and trees. Nonrenewable resources are those that take millions of years to form or do not get replaced once they have been used. The minerals found in the Peruvian Andes are examples of nonrenewable resources.

Over the years, people have been using Earth's resources rapidly. Many nonrenewable resources are running out. Many renewable resources have been used up faster than they can be replaced. People need to conserve these resources if they are to last into the future.

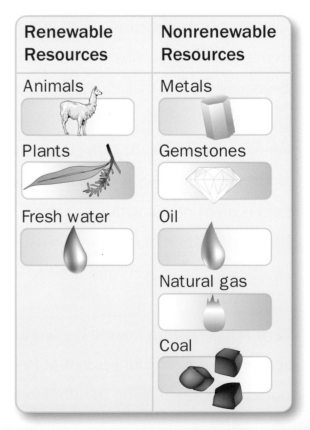

Renewable Resources	Nonrenewable Resources
Animals	Metals
Plants	Gemstones
Fresh water	Oil
	Natural gas
	Coal

Conservation Conservation is the careful use of a resource to save it for the future. Conservation can reduce the amount of a resource taken from the environment. Conservation also includes the protection of areas where resources are at risk of depletion.

conservation
protection and careful use of natural resources

Some areas of the Peruvian Andes have suffered **deforestation**. Deforestation is the clearing of forest areas. Although trees are a renewable resource, they still take many years to grow to full size. Regrowth cannot always keep up with the rate at which many forests are cut down. In Peru, trees have been cut down for timber or cleared for mining, farming, or building settlements. Peru is losing its trees for making medicines like quinine.

Conservation efforts by the Peruvian government include the establishment of several national parks in which trees are protected. One park is the Yanachaga-Chemillen National Park, which has a large cloud forest area. Another park is the Manu National Park, which includes some of the foothill rain forests of the Andes.

Green-winged macaws in Manu National Park

Recycling Another way people can help save resources is by **recycling**. Recycling is the collection, processing, and reuse of materials that would otherwise be thrown away. Recycling conserves natural resources by reusing old products and reducing the need for new material.

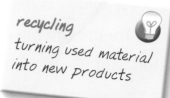

recycling
turning used material into new products

Copper is one resource from Peru's mountains that can be recycled. Copper has an endless recyclable life. Copper, or any of its alloys such as bronze, can be melted and reused over and over again. Electric cables and wires contain copper, so these are often recycled. Copper from hot water systems, pipes, or old car parts can also be recycled. Copper is also often recovered from old computer parts for recycling.

Used copper pipes compressed for recycling

Recycling materials can also be a way to make money. Recycled copper is worth about as much as newly mined copper.

Think about what you read. Think about the maps and diagrams. Use these to answer the questions. Share what you think with others.

1. Name two or more resources from the country you read about in this book.

2. Name at least three ways the natural resources discussed in this book are used.

3. Explain the difference between a renewable resource and a nonrenewable resource.

4. Give at least two examples of how people can conserve Earth's resources.

VISUAL LITERACY

Resource Map

A resource map shows you the natural resources found in an area.
Resource maps often use symbols to show where the different kinds of resources are found.

Resource maps can show different kinds of resources.
Look back at the resource map on page 9. It shows where minerals are found in Peru's mountains. The map on page 19 is also a resource map. It shows the main mineral deposits around the world.

How to Read a Resource Map

1. **Read the title.**
   The title tells you which kinds of resources will be shown and in which area.

2. **Read the key.**
   The key tells you what the different symbols represent.

3. **Study the map.**
   Find the symbols on the map to see which resources are found in which areas.

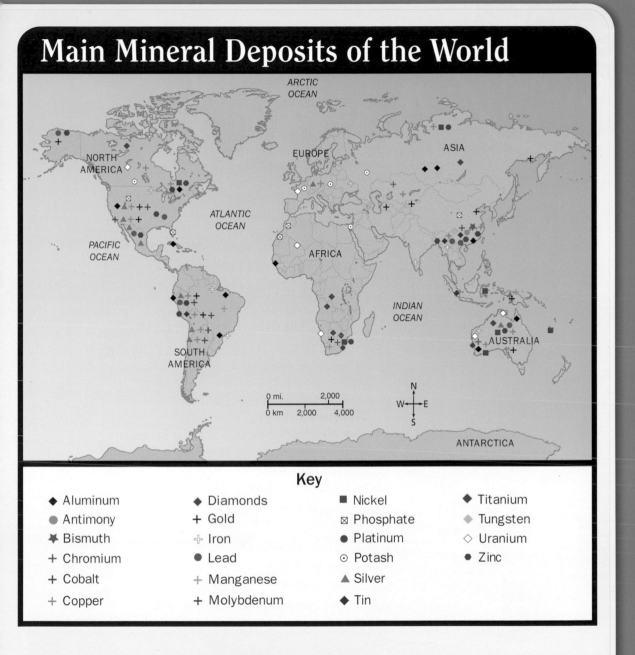

Main Mineral Deposits of the World

Key

◆ Aluminum	◆ Diamonds	■ Nickel	◆ Titanium
● Antimony	+ Gold	⊠ Phosphate	◆ Tungsten
✳ Bismuth	✦ Iron	● Platinum	◇ Uranium
+ Chromium	● Lead	⊙ Potash	● Zinc
+ Cobalt	+ Manganese	▲ Silver	
+ Copper	+ Molybdenum	◆ Tin	

What's on the Map?

Read the map by following the directions on page 18. Then answer the following questions. Which areas are rich in mineral resources? Which areas do not have mineral deposits? What mineral deposits can be found near the area where you live?

Problem-Solution Article

A problem-solution article describes a problem and gives possible solutions to the problem. The problem-solution article beginning on page 21 describes the problem of environmental damage in Peru's Andes.

A problem-solution article usually contains the following:

The Introduction
The introduction outlines the problem.

The Problem
The first body paragraphs explain how the problem came about.

The Solutions
The next body paragraphs give some possible solutions to the problem.

Saving the Mountains in Peru

The mountain ranges of the Andes are among the most diverse regions on Earth. The lowlands are covered with dense tropical forests with numerous trees. The higher regions are covered with cloud forests that contain a large variety of ferns and orchids.

However, farming and mining are destroying large parts of these mountain ranges. Nearly 90 percent of mountain forests have disappeared from the Andes. Many mountains that were once covered with forests now have just small patches of green. These forests could all be gone within the next ten years.

The forests provide a home for many rare animals such as jaguars, pumas, and mountain tapirs. The mountain tapir is at risk of extinction because of the destruction of its habitat in the Andes. Only about 200 mountain tapirs can be found in Peru today.

The **title** tells you the topic of the article.

The **introduction** outlines the problem.

Photographs support the facts in the text.

Mountain tapir

The Problem: Environmental Damage

There are two main ways that the environment in the Peruvian Andes has been damaged. These are deforestation and pollution.

Deforestation

Deforestation, the cutting down or burning of forests, is a major problem in Peru's mountains. Many farmers clear mountain forests for land. They use the land to grow crops, such as potatoes, corn, and coffee, and to graze their cattle. In the 1970s and 1980s, thousands of hectares of forests in the Andes were cleared.

Over time, crops use up many nutrients in the mountain soil. Many mountain trees cannot survive in the poor soil. Some are in danger of dying out. For example, there are fewer quenual trees. Today, these trees are found on only 2 percent of the area they once covered.

> The first body paragraphs explain how the **problem** came about.

Cutting trees for timber and firewood has added to the deforestation problem. The roots of forest trees hold the soil in place. When many mountain trees are cut down, landslides can occur. In 1987, heavy rains caused large landslides in Peru's Huallaga Valley. Many people lost their homes.

Deforestation in the Peruvian Andes

Children play in a polluted environment outside a metal processing plant in La Oroya, Peru.

Pollution

Peru's mountains also face problems of pollution. The mountains contain a wealth of minerals, such as gold, copper, silver, lead, and zinc. Mining provides a large income for Peru's economy. However, large-scale mining has caused pollution.

In the mining process, people use chemicals, such as mercury, to remove minerals from rock. If these chemicals get spilled, they can pollute underground water, rivers, and streams. The chemicals spread to plants that absorb this water. They can also affect animals and people who eat the plants or drink the water. Mercury can damage people's and animals' brains, nerves, and kidneys.

Gold is one mineral that is usually extracted from rocks with mercury. In 2000, a large amount of mercury was spilled near the Yanacocha gold mine in the northern Peruvian Andes. Many streams in the region are now polluted as a result.

Mining factories also release gases that cause air pollution. The gases combine with water vapor in the air and produce chemicals called acids. The acid then falls back onto Earth with rain as acid rain. Many trees and other plants die when they absorb acid rainwater. Mining in the town of La Oroya in the Andes has polluted the air with poisonous chemicals. A large number of plants in the area have been destroyed by acid rain.

The Solutions

The next body paragraphs give some possible **solutions** to the problem.

Mountain regions are crucial for the health of the planet. There are several solutions to the problems they face. These include creating national parks to protect threatened mountain areas. Using safe mining methods and following strict mining laws are also ways to solve the problem.

The Huascaran National Park, which was created in 1975, is one example. The park covers a large number of mountain peaks, glaciers, and rivers in its 340,000 hectares (840,000 acres). It provides a safe habitat for a large variety of plant and animal species.

National Parks

One way to preserve mountains and their forests from the harmful effects of farming, logging, and mining is to create national parks. A national park is an area set aside to protect the natural environment. Plants and animals in national parks are protected from human activities. Peru's government has already made several national parks in the Andes to protect them from further damage.

A lake and mountains in the Huascaran National Park

Better Farming Methods

Illegal farming caused a huge amount of deforestation in Peru in the 1970s and 1980s.

People living in the mountains are being encouraged to use safe methods of farming, such as terrace farming. Terrace farming uses steps on mountain slopes to reduce the amount of soil that gets washed downhill with rainwater.

Safe Mining

One solution to reduce pollution caused by mining is to have strict rules for mining companies to clear up dumps of waste. Many mining companies in Peru are already making an effort to reduce the harmful effects of pollution. They follow mining methods that cut down on polluting dust. Some mining companies have planted hundreds of plants in areas where plants have been destroyed by mine pollution. Waste water released from mines is treated to counter the effect of poisonous chemicals. There are also procedures in place to clean up any spills.

Terrace farming on a hillside in Peru

Conservation

Industry representatives and the government are getting together to solve the problems caused by deforestation and mining. Recently, an International Year of Mountains was declared. Many countries across the world began projects to protect mountains such as the Andes from environmental damage.

Local people contribute to this effort by conserving mountain resources such as wood, water, and minerals.

People have realized that it is important to protect the diversity of life in the Andes Mountains. If enough effort is made to protect and conserve the mountain environment, important mountain resources will still be available to people in the future.

Preparing trees for planting in the Peruvian Andes

Apply the Key Concepts

Key Concept 1 Earth provides many natural resources that people can use.

Activity

Write a list of four things that you use every day, such as kinds of food or clothing. Then write down the natural resources that these things come from. For example, they might come from plants or animals.

1. Wool sweater: wool comes from sheep

2. Apples: grow on trees

3.

Key Concept 2 Different resources are useful to people in different ways.

Activity

Create a chart with three columns. In the first column, name some resources found in Peru's mountains. In the second column, name the special properties of each natural resource. In the third column, name the ways people use each natural resource.

Resource	Properties	Uses

Key Concept 3 Conservation and recycling can help save resources.

Activity

Write a short letter to a conservation group. Give two reasons why you think Peru's mountains should be conserved. Give one suggestion for how people can help conserve the mountains.

To whom it may concern:
_____
_____
_____
_____

Write Your Own Problem-Solution Article

You have read the problem-solution article about environmental damage in Peru. Now you can write your own problem-solution article.

1. Study the Model

Look back at pages 21–26. Read the labels to find the important features of a problem-solution article. What information is presented in the introduction section of the article? What information is presented in *The Problem* section of the article? What information is presented in *The Solutions* section of the article?

Writing a Problem-Solution Article

◆ Choose a topic related to conservation. The topic must have a problem and possible solutions.

◆ Write an introduction explaining what needs to be conserved.

◆ Write several body paragraphs describing the problem.

◆ Write several more paragraphs giving some solutions to the problem.

2. Choose Your Topic

Now you can choose your topic. Your topic will be a conservation issue. It must involve a problem for which there are possible solutions. You may choose an animal that is at risk of dying out. You may choose an area where the natural environment is at risk. You may already know of a conservation cause that you would like to research. Otherwise, look on the Internet and through books and magazines to get some ideas.

3. Research Your Topic

Write down notes on what you already know about your topic. Organize them into columns labeled "Problem" and "Solution." Then think about what else you will need to find out. Remember that you will need to discuss the conservation problem in the first section. In the second section, you will need to present some possible solutions to the problem.

Topic: Giant Pandas

Problem	Solution
Habitat destruction	Protect the bamboo forests

Make a list of questions. Use this list to guide your research. Then look through books and magazines. Go on the Internet. Take notes on what you find out and add them to your chart. Make copies of pictures you may want to use.

4. Write a Draft

Now you can write a draft of your article. Look back at the article on pages 21–26. Use it as a model for writing your article.

5. Revise and Edit

Read your draft. Check to see that it is well organized. Keep your research nearby so you can check that all the facts are correct. Look for any words that are misspelled. Make sure that each sentence starts with a capital letter.

Create a Conservation Poster

Now you can share your work. You can design a poster about your conservation cause. Then you can share your poster with the rest of the class.

How to Make a Poster

1. Think of a slogan.
A slogan is a catchy phrase. It sums up your conservation goal, for example, "Save the Pandas." Write your slogan in big letters on your poster paper.

2. Include a strong photograph or illustration.
Use a copy of a photograph you found during your research. Or draw an illustration on your poster. The photograph or illustration should show the animal or natural environment that you want to conserve.

3. Write some information about the cause.
Write a short paragraph about your animal or natural environment. Tell why it needs to be conserved. Give important facts. For example, you could write the number of pandas alive today compared to 50 years ago. Keep your sentences short and to the point.

4. Share your work.
Hang all the class posters on the classroom wall. As a class, walk around the room and read each other's posters. Be prepared to answer any questions your classmates may have about your conservation cause.

Glossary

alloy – a mix of two or more metals

altitudes – heights from sea level

conductor – a material that easily transmits heat or electricity

conservation – protection and careful use of natural resources

deforestation – the burning or cutting down of forests

depleted – reduced over time

deposits – layers of a mineral or fuel in or on Earth

malleable – soft and easy to mold into different shapes

minerals – solid materials that can be dug out of the ground

natural resources – materials that are found in nature and are useful to people

nonrenewable – not able to be replaced once it is used

properties – special features or qualities

quinine – a medicine made from the bark of the cinchona tree and used to treat malaria

recycling – turning used material into new products

renewable – able to be replaced by nature once it is used

replenished – replaced or created again

tropics – the area between the Tropic of Cancer and the Tropic of Capricorn

Index